Adages and Aphorisms from Philosophilus *

*Philosophical musings of a curmudgeonly philosopher of the old Athenian school.

Adages and Aphorisms From Philosophilus

Written and Illustrated
By Richard O. Calkins

Published by  A Different Perception

Our mission is to provide new and useful insights to expand our perceptions of the human condition, art, society and the universe in which we live.

Copyright © 2014 by Richard O. Calkins

All rights reserved, including the right to reproduce this book or any portion thereof in any form whatsoever without permission in writing from the publisher, except by a reviewer who quotes brief passages in a review presented in a magazine, newspaper or broadcast. For information, contact Calkins Publishing Company LLC at info@calkinspublishing.com.

First edition

Library of Congress catalog card number: 2011937520

ISBN: 978-0-9836770-1-7

To my wife Beth and my daughters Trina and Teresa. May you always have the same joy in your lives as you have brought into mine.

Other Books by Richard O. Calkins

Relativity Revisited - 2011

Oneliners - Coming Soon

TABLE OF CONTENTS

Introduction	1
On Human Nature and the Human Condition	3
On Human Relations	11
On Wisdom or its Absence	21
On Politics, Government and Diplomacy	25
On Commerce and Finance	33
On the Law	39
On Education and Success	43
On Creativity and Art	49
On Gastronomy and Imbibition	53
On Health and Medicine	57
On Science and Technology	61
On Cosmology	69
On the Meaning of Life	73
On This and That	79

Introduction

Philosophilus is an ancient Athenian philosopher and curmudgeon reputedly being channeled by a man named Richard Calkins. Mr. Calkins, for some unknown reason, lives in a bucolic hamlet in the State of Washington. It has been said that the channeling is facilitated by the fact that Mr. Calkins is as much a curmudgeon as is Philosophilus himself.

During their discourses, Philosophilus has learned much about modern times from Mr. Calkins. Not surprisingly, Philosophilus does not approve of most of what he has learned; but then, he doesn't approve of much of anything.

Presented here are excerpts from Mr. Calkins's many conversations with Philosophilus over the years. They range from Philosophilus's observations of ancient times to his opinions about the foibles of modern man with some asides on the history in between. Throughout, they are flavored by a world view formed in ancient times by this curmudgeonly philosopher.

Within these pages you will find that which you love and that which you hate, for the truths which some men revere are despised by others.

Philosophilus

One must take care not to mistake curmudgeonly irreverence for disbelief. A careful examination of irreverence will detect traces of humor and affection. It takes a believer to be irreverent.

Philosophilus

But one also should not mistake belief for unquestioning approval.

Philosophilus

On Human Nature and the Human Condition

Over the vast panorama of history, human nature has proven to be remarkably resistant to change. This can be deeply distressing when dwelt upon.

Philosophilus

Dogs are open, exuberant, playful, disorderly, love unconditionally and are much beloved by men.

Cats are secretive, quiet, play with their claws out, fastidious, love reservedly if at all and are much beloved by women.

Whatever might be learned from this is certain to violate political correctitude.

Philosophilus

It may well be true, as alleged by the young, that the old have only a dim and feeble memory of their youth; but the young have no basis for even imagining the circumstances of being old.

Philosophilus

An open mind, as a virtue unto itself, is vastly overrated.

An open mind that is not buttressed by judgment, to tell the bad from the good, and by integrity, to prefer the good to the bad, leads to chaos and corruption.

Philosophilus

If you have a mind of your own, get used to being out of step and unpopular.

Philosophilus

It is the misfortune of mankind that goodness and greatness are, at best, uncorrelated.

Philosophilus

There are two kinds of people who sleep soundly at night: those who are financially secure and those who are innocent. If you should want to know how many people that is, I can only advise you that the whole is precisely equal to the sum of the parts.

    Philosophilus

Some people complain because they didn't get what they deserve.

Others complain because they did.

    Philosophilus

Every last one of us is willing to try something new, provided the consequences of not doing so are sufficiently dire.

    Philosophilus

If you think yawning is contagious, try vomiting.

    Philosophilus

It has been said that man must dearly love earthquakes, mud slides, hurricanes, volcanic eruptions and floods since so many of his most desirable properties are located where these events frequently occur.

On that basis, it is abundantly clear that man thoroughly detests tornados.

Philosophilus

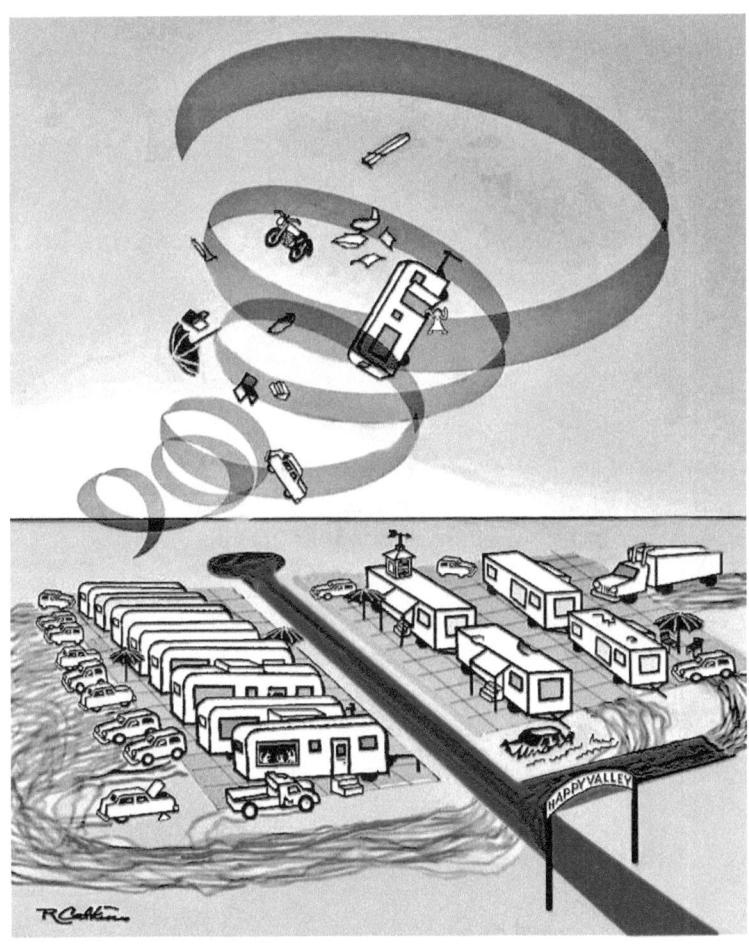

A surprise is something we did not anticipate that happens when we least expect it.

The pleasant surprise is a myth.

                Philosophilus

Wishful thinking may make you happy, but it will not keep you happy.

Nor will much else.

                Philosophilus

Every man loves truth, faith, fidelity and virtue, provided they are at a comfortable distance.

                Philosophilus

When faced with a dangerous emergency, chickens run in all directions at once, ostriches bury their heads, parrots shriek and dodos were wont to stand about and gawk.

People, being more versatile than birds, have managed to master all four of these stratagems.

                Philosophilus

To dare to dream great dreams is to risk great disappointments. These can be painful. But to not dream great dreams is to assure a life of mediocrity. One can overcome disappointments and dream again. Mediocrity is hard to overcome and far less likely to lead to happiness.

Philosophilus

A zealot is one who knows with absolute certainty that which he knows without ever having had to think about it.

Philosophilus

On Human Relations

If you laud an opponent's idea with enough profusion, he will be thrown off balance long enough for you to think of a way to refute it.

    Philosophilus

Contrary to popular belief, swearing at the drivers of other vehicles will neither impress them nor improve their driving.

    Philosophilus

Some peoples have managed to avoid the pitfalls of nationalism and simply battle between tribes.

    Philosophilus

If you always expect the best of everyone, you will always be unprepared when you get the worst.

Philosophilus

Attacks invariably are made by the strong against the weak, never by the weak against the strong. To be weak is to invite attack.

Philosophilus

An expert is someone who may understand less than others but can cite more references.

Experts are best avoided.

Philosophilus

If people respond to you by speaking slowly while smiling with great compassion, you may want to elevate the intellectual level of your discourse.

On the other hand, what you're doing avoids a lot of arguments.

Philosophilus

He who avoids controversy by ignoring its existence sows the seeds of raging conflict.

Philosophilus

Your very best is all anyone can expect you to do, but to have to assert that you have done your very best, even when true, is not a good thing.

Philosophilus

An extremist is one who believes that if shouting at a man with whom he disagrees is a good thing, then slaughtering that man and his family and his friends and his community and his nation is an even better one.

Give wide berth to extremists.

Philosophilus

Telling someone what to do is more appreciated by the teller than by the tellee.

Philosophilus

Some men think deeply and speak both quietly and rarely. Other men speak loudly and often but think not at all. The latter have a greater impact on human affairs than the former.

Philosophilus

No assessment of your endeavors is as sincere as that which one delivers from his purse.

Philosophilus

The hero who goes in harm's way to protect his community does great service to his fellow citizens, if only by allowing them the opportunity to criticize his performance without having to undertake any effort or risk to themselves.

Philosophilus

If you think of a new idea, by the time you get people to accept it, it not only will no longer be new, but it will have become so familiar to so many that no one will believe it was you who thought of it.

    Philosophilus

No one is more boring than an intelligent person who has focused his entire being on becoming the consummate expert on a single subject, unless it's a stupid person who has done the same thing.

    Philosophilus

It is the rare man indeed who extends the same measure of loyalty, devotion, trust, patience, protectiveness and dependability to his dog as the dog routinely extends to his master. Which of the two possesses greater nobility of spirit is abundantly clear.

    Philosophilus

Young men are full of energy and impatience. They just can't wait to get out there and set the world on fire. Older, more experienced men have learned that the world does not want to be set on fire.

    Philosophilus

In ancient times, a tyrant, two senators, a high priest, several attorneys and a number of bureaucrats from a town near Athens went on safari in deepest Africa. They were set upon and devoured by a savage tribe of wild cannibals. Every year, on the anniversary of that event, the citizens of the town take a large basket of tribute to the cannibals in gratitude.

Philosophilus

Silence is golden, but isn't for children.

Philosophilus

It has been said that the way to a man's heart is through his stomach. It might equally be said that the way to a woman's heart is for him to crawl on it.

Philosophilus

Free men can be lead but cannot be driven.

          Philosophilus

A good leader is one who can persuade his followers that they are the ones who determined what needs to be done, that they will benefit from doing it, and that they have the drive and wherewithal to accomplish it.

          Philosophilus

A great leader is one who can make his followers believe that achieving greatness is inherent in their nature.

          Philosophilus

The quality of a man's character is better determined by observing his enemies than by observing his friends.

          Philosophilus

If you tend to go back and forth on everything, you often will just end up wherever it was that you started.

          Philosophilus

One of the most effective forms of leadership is setting a good example. It is unfortunate that it is so seldom used.

          Philosophilus

Men are terrified of women who refer to the Almighty as "She." Those who have lived with one know it to be with good reason.

Philosophilus

In a crisis, the man who instantly shouts with conviction "Run off that cliff!" is more often obeyed than the man who pauses for a moment to think on it.

Philosophilus

It may be customary for most things to go in and out of fashion, but that should not include truth, honor, wisdom, thought, integrity, courage or compassion.

Philosophilus

On Wisdom or its Absence

Just because modern men live in the present and their forebears lived in the dim and distant past does not mean that they are either wiser or more knowledgeable than their forebears. Anyone who thinks otherwise has administered neither a test of intelligence nor one of history to the average citizen.

Philosophilus

There are some people who are so determinedly stupid that they gather into large groups where each one attempts to demonstrate that he is stupider than the others.

We call them demonstrators.

Philosophilus

You can take comfort in the knowledge that everyone does something stupid once in a while. The trick lies in not doing it all the while.

Philosophilus

One of the greatest impediments to the achievement of wisdom is a high esteem for one's own intellect.

Philosophilus

A wise man is one who has learned from experience to embrace that which is good and avoid that which is bad.

A man can become wise without having great intelligence.

A man can have great intelligence without becoming wise.

Philosophilus

When someone lauds you for having a mind like a steel trap, remember that steel does not think.

Philosophilus

On Politics, Government and Diplomacy

A democratic republic is a nation that is founded on the charmingly innocent notion that its citizens will take turns holding high office.

Philosophilus

There is a heated debate raging between those who believe that man is causing a phenomenon called global warming and those who do not. The latter are producing and consuming energy in myriad ways. The former are all buying SUVs with climate control.

Philosophilus

The reason so many politicians blow with the wind is because it is so often rewarded by the electorate.

Philosophilus

Only the hopelessly muddled would believe that you can dissuade with diplomacy one who lusts for your blood.

Philosophilus

If you can't dance, can't sing, can't cipher, can't scribe, can't sow, can't reap, can't lead, can't follow, can't plan, can't build, can't cogitate, can't be honest and are immune to logic, you can always run for high political office.

Philosophilus

A liberal readily adopts any manner of new ideas. A conservative, on the other hand, has already adopted his ideas.

Philosophilus

A diplomat is one who can deliver a mortal insult without offending its recipient.

Philosophilus

A canny monarch knows better than to send a diplomat to deliver a well-deserved insult to a fellow tyrant. However, should your monarch be seeking someone to perform that service, anyone who is adequate to the task should take care to be occupied elsewhere.

Philosophilus

No tyrant is harder to dislodge than the military hero who volunteers himself to save his countrymen from the avarice of their elected officials.

Philosophilus

Liberals and conservatives no longer listen to each other, and with good reason. Each already knows what the other is going to say and knows it to be wrong.

Philosophilus

A politician's respect for our esteem is so great that he will spend any amount of the wealth of others to attain it -- unless he thinks we can be bamboozled by empty promises.

Philosophilus

A conservative may seek to discourage utterances that he believes are harmful to society. A liberal, however, can be relied upon to zealously defend our freedom of speech, unless he thinks we will say something lacking political correctitude.

Philosophilus

A conservative is one who believes that the law should apply equally to all, no matter how painful the result. A liberal is one who thinks the application of law should avoid causing pain, even to the law-breaker, no matter how inconsistent the result.

          Philosophilus

There are those who call themselves republicans and proclaim their reverence for the republic. There are those who call themselves democrats and proclaim their reverence for democracy. They fight with each other incessantly. It appears that what we need is some republicrats.

On the other hand, they'd probably just fight with the democlicans.

          Philosophilus

It seems that the benefit of giving political groups names is so that one can know which ones to oppose and which to support without the bother of having to listen to them.

          Philosophilus

What now is called economics once was called political economy. The name was changed when it became clear that nothing political was related to economy.

          Philosophilus

A statesman is one who has mastered the art of receiving credit for great happenings while concurrently avoiding blame for their unintended consequences.

        Philosophilus

Ancient Athens, being a democracy, was a place of extraordinary sensitivity to the sensibilities of others. For example, citizens going forth into the streets with their canines took along slaves to pick up the droppings. However, even in a democracy, sensitivity for others can be overdone. In Athens, we became beset with troublemakers who opposed any utterance that might offend their fragile sensibilities. They even persuaded those in authority to forbid certain kinds of speech that they found to be offensive, wrapping their arguments in the veils of something called political correctitude. Even Socrates was not immune to their machinations.

        Philosophilus

I understand that in modern times people of wisdom have enshrined freedom of speech into your very Constitution, taking care to omit any considerations for political correctitude. I am concerned, however, that some in your nation's highest court are of such fragile sensibilities as to have found penumbras* of political correctitude in the darker crevices of that document. Socratists beware!

        Philosophilus

* *Or was that perambulations?*

Trying to lead a populace comprised of liberals, conservatives, independents, libertarians, the old, the young, doctors, patients, lawyers, clients, businessmen, white collar workers, blue collar workers, industrialists, unionists, shopkeepers, teachers, students, farmers, landlords, renters, homeowners, Catholics, protestants, Muslims, Jews, agnostics, atheists, dreamers, realists, bureaucrats, taxpayers, welfare recipients, producers, consumers, the practical, the impractical, the compassionate, the indifferent, the greedy, the altruistic, the committed, the uncommitted, urbanites, suburbanites, rurals, drivers, pedestrians, bicyclists, capitalists, socialists, people who look ahead, people who live for the moment, parents, non-parents, singles, married couples, drinkers, abstainers, and assorted others makes herding cats seem pleasant and productive.

Philosophilus

Most men assert that their choice of leader is not greatly important because they are too wise to be misled by an aberrant one. That leads one to wonder why the Germans followed Hitler, the Japanese followed Tojo, the Chinese followed Mao Tse Tung, the Serbs followed Milosevic, the Transylvanians followed Vlad the Impaler, the Mongols followed Attila the Hun, the North Koreans followed Kim Ill Wind, the Soviets followed Stalin, the ...

Philosophilus

On Commerce and Finance

No matter how thoroughly nor with what devotion one performs the tasks assigned to his job, that does not constitute doing the job. The job is done only by fulfilling its purpose.

>Philosophilus

Gambling is said to be a zero sum game, since every drachma one gambler wins another must lose. In contrast, we are told that the market for financial securities is a positive sum game, since so many can win from the same transactions. In line to benefit from this largess, we are told, are stockbrokers, fund managers, securities analysts and investors.

Three out of four is not bad.

>Philosophilus

There are those who have the daring to bet their financial means on the forecasts of experts, and there are those who do not. The former are called courageous and visionary investors. The latter are called solvent.

>Philosophilus

Management would be a far more tolerable occupation if it weren't for having to deal with all those irritating people.

>Philosophilus

An economist is a sort of wizard who can predict with absolute certainty that there is a major business downturn in our future. He'd be far more impressive if he had a clue as to when it will happen and what will cause it.

Philosophilus

Don't listen to economists.

Even economists don't listen to economists.

Philosophilus

I understand that the tyrants in charge of modern business emporiums expect their minions to do many things at once. Apparently, this is called multitasking. It must be extremely difficult to multitask with a monotask mind.

Philosophilus

If that which you can do is something done by others, you have the difficult task of convincing an employer that you are the one to hire.

If it is something not done by others, you have the difficult task of convincing an employer that what you do has value.

No one said that getting a job would be easy.

Philosophilus

Man's obsession with knowing the unknowable has led many to enter the arcane and mysterious order of forecasters. It turns out that the benefit of having a forecast is that it allows us to determine whether we are above it or below it.

Philosophilus

There are those who believe that the exchange of payment for the use of money is not within the bounds of acceptable behavior. Such people usually are found in undeveloped countries.

Philosophilus

Some people claim that you get what you pay for. But the only thing you can count on is that you'll pay for what you get.

Philosophilus

Notwithstanding what tasks you do to secure your living or the skill with which you do them, the day will come when you can no longer carry on. What happens then will be determined by the preparations you have made against that day.

Philosophilus

The grasshopper spends the golden days of summer in constant feasting and abundant living, but perishes when the approach of winter finds him unprepared.

The bee, through constant diligence, builds a sturdy hive and stocks it with honey, such that he can hunker down throughout the bleak and dismal winter and emerge to resume his endless tasks in the spring.

By spending every waking moment bent to his tasks, it might be said that the bee never really lived. The grasshopper, on the other hand, had a glorious summer of joyous abandon and exuberant living. Who is to say which of them made the better choice?

Philosophilus

If you happen to be a grasshopper, make really good friends with a bee.

If you happen to be a bee, beware the blandishments of grasshoppers.

Philosophilus

On the Law

It has been said that a man is only as good as his word. It equally can be said that his word is only as good as the man.

Philosophilus

A contract, on the other hand, is as good as the lawyer who wrote it, the lawyer hired to overturn it, the judge who adjudicates it, the jury that hears the case, the witnesses hired to defend it, the witnesses hired to refute it and the sheriff sent out to enforce it.

Philosophilus

No defendant is more vehemently admonished than one who has injured an assailant while defending himself.

Philosophilus

An attorney is a scoundrel who has learned how to garner wealth by promoting the misery of others while avoiding any penalty to himself.

Beware of attorneys.

Philosophilus

In the aftermath of a vicious assault, most men will demand an accounting of the perpetrator, whereas a defense attorney will demand to know from the victim what he did to provoke the attack.

Beware of defense attorneys.

Unless they happen to be yours.

Even then, be careful.

> *Philosophilus*

On Education and Success

Children have a natural talent to think creatively and to bring their unique points of view to bear on interacting with the universe.

We send them all to school to train them to think and act alike.

           Philosophilus

There are those who say we learn by doing. But if this were so, how did we learn the doing?

           Philosophilus

Some teachers favor the stick. Others, claiming to be wiser, favor the carrot. But it is inarguable that you can strike a recalcitrant student more soundly with the stick.

           Philosophilus

It is very important for a prospective teacher to learn how to teach, but not nearly as important as for him to learn what to teach.

           Philosophilus

No matter the depth of our antipathy for studying the subject, life requires even the most reluctant of us to be master practitioners of organic chemistry.

Philosophilus

I am told that modern educators have invented new ways to teach mathematics that relieve students of the boredom of memorizing multiplication tables and long hours of practicing addition and subtraction. This allows them to concentrate on the broader concepts of mathematics rather than merely practicing its mechanics.

Shopkeepers who hire these students have responded to their new abilities by installing machines for handling transactions that automatically enter the price of each item, total all the prices, calculate and add the emperor's taxes, assess the patron's remittance and tell the employee how much change to pay.

Philosophilus

The greatest success a man can have is not to be found in the size of his mansion, the wealth of his possessions, or even in the accomplishments to be lauded in his obituary, but simply that he can come to his death bed without regrets.

There are few great successes in life.

Philosophilus

If you have passed through life without ever having caused a change in human affairs of sufficient magnitude as to incur the wrath of others, you have accomplished little.

Philosophilus

It's okay to look back on your accomplishments from time to time, but, to secure your future, you really must bother to look ahead.

Philosophilus

If you never fail, you aren't trying hard enough to master new skills. On the other hand, if, when you fail, you keep getting up and trying the same thing over again, you are a slow learner.

Philosophilus

Success in commerce comes to he who tries harder than the others, even if only marginally.

Philosophilus

When, after diligent effort, we attain such expertise that we are fully satisfied with our performance, we cease to grow.

Philosophilus

A journalist is someone who has spent many years in prestigious educational institutions learning how to write while managing to avoid exposure to whatever it is he will write about.

Be careful of what you learn from a journalist.

Be especially careful of what you tell a journalist.

      Philosophilus

The thoughts which can enhance our knowledge are to be found only among those with which we do not already agree.

      Philosophilus

Those who have lost their ambition usually have done so simply by not moving fast enough to keep up with it.

      Philosophilus

On Creativity and Art

An artist makes many subtle adjustments to his paintings to improve the quality of the final work. The writer edits the text of his masterpiece constantly to improve the flow of his plot. Yet both commonly find that the first attempt was by far the best, having an essence that cannot later be recaptured.

Can you say, "Quit while you're ahead?"

        Philosophilus

The student carefully paints a tree on his canvas and it looks like blobs of paint. The master casually strokes blobs of paint on his canvas and it looks, for all the world, like a tree.

        Philosophilus

The study of art can teach us many things. For example, red mixed with yellow produces the brilliant orange of the sunset. Yellow mixed with blue produces the verdant greens of the woodlands. Blue mixed with red produces mauve. Yuk!

        Philosophilus

The artist who paints for sustenance is better served by winning the People's Choice award from the unwashed masses than the expert Jurors award for best in show.

        Philosophilus

Artistic genius at work is a profoundly messy thing.

Philosophilus

The sun, which is orange, turns the sky blue. The moon and stars, which are white, turn the sky black. Go figure.

Philosophilus

Should you happen to study the arcane and infuriating pastime called watercolor painting, you will encounter what its practitioners call the happy accident. The happy accident is said to be an inherent benefit of the medium's unpredictability that can greatly enhance the charm of your paintings. The difference between a happy accident and an unhappy accident apparently is determined by whether or not you can figure out how to recover from it.

Philosophilus

Artists can be an abhorrent lot. Realists abhor ambiguity. Impressionists abhor crisp edges. Pastellists abhor clean hands. Watercolorists abhor dry paper. Oil painters abhor fresh air. Abstract artists abhor being understood. Cubists abhor being mistaken for abstract artists.

Philosophilus

On Gastronomy and Imbibition

You can have your cake and eat it too. What you cannot do is eat your cake and have it too.

Philosophilus

The amount of intoxicant one believes he can hold without impairing his faculties is much affected by the amount he has already consumed.

Philosophilus

It is my understanding that the Celts in the wilds of Britannia greatly enjoy a festival where each man attempts to hurl the trunk of a tree as far as he can. I am convinced that a festival I have heard of in a town called Munich would be more appealing.

Philosophilus

One of the problems we faced in the ancient world was the need to control our ingestion of intoxicants at a festival. Lacking modern-day wagons that drive themselves, we had to retain the competence to walk home after the festivities.

Philosophilus

There are few experiences more intoxicating than finding oneself at a festival with a free bar.

Philosophilus

With the far flung spread of commerce in ancient Athens, we were introduced to many new things that became highly esteemed by the populace. One of these was the delightful eating establishment called the Chinese restaurant.

The Chinese restaurant most popular in Athens offered a diverse cornucopia of exotic edibles. Despite the excellence of their food, they were surprisingly inexpensive. Their least expensive offering was a meal called "The Buddhist Monk's Delight." It consisted of a cup of tea and a begging bowl to take around to the other tables.

Philosophilus

A secret the Chinese do not share with Occidentals is that they eat by holding the bowl up to their mouths and using the chopsticks to shovel in food. They are much amused by people who try to pick things up with them.

Philosophilus

On Health and Medicine

As we grow older, it becomes more important to train ourselves to think of dropping something as a delightful opportunity for beneficial exercise. Not only is this good for our morale, but, for many of us, it's the only exercise we get.

Philosophilus

Physicians are highly trained practitioners of the healing arts who have learned to read the subtle nuances of our immensely complex human body to diagnose that which ails us.

Sometimes they are right.

Philosophilus

No medical practitioner is better versed in his art than the elderly gerontologist.

Philosophilus

Some philosophers, in an effort to divine the cause of our illnesses, have concocted the theory that they are caused by little, tiny organisms that are too small for us to see. Logic tells us that this is patently ridiculous.

For example, many illnesses are fatal. In order to kill us, these hypothetical organisms would have to be better fitted for survival than are we. However, they could not be better fitted for survival with intelligence so inferior to ours. But by killing us, they also seal their own doom. With our larger brains and greater power for reasoning, we would never commit such a stupid blunder.

While we're on the subject, how is mother earth doing these days?

Philosophilus

If, in your efforts to seek release from stress, someone suggests that you may be a tad unbalanced, take heart. Psychiatrists don't know nearly as much as they'd like you to think they do.

Philosophilus

On Science and Technology

Throughout history, man has created better conveyances and more efficient tools to do his work with less call for his own energy. This has provided more and more time for meaningless exercise to maintain his physical being.

We call that progress.

            Philosophilus

I understand that the newest magic is a thing called nanotechnology. Its practitioners are busily making everything smaller and smaller at such a furious pace they must think we will part with good money in return for nothing at all.

            Philosophilus

We are told that the new cannot be trusted because it has not withstood the test of time; but, that which has withstood the test of time is obsolete. This must be another one of those infernal conundrums.

            Philosophilus

One can lead a horse to the water supply, but must not allow it to relieve itself there.

We call that ecological science.

        Philosophilus

I hear there is a new wizardry that makes magical devices to overcome your loss of hearing as you grow older. One such device even has a tiny control you can carry in the folds of your toga that will control the loudness of what you hear. Despite its apparent advantages, I strongly urge you to avoid the ones that have such a control. You'll only end up quarreling with your spouse over who gets to carry it. "You aren't listening, dear. Can you hear me now?"

        Philosophilus

Television is a creation of the black arts in which movement substitutes for discourse, rapid framing substitutes for thought and a flat rectangle substitutes for the vast expanse of the universe.

        Philosophilus

Scientists are often their own worst enemies. For example, botanists call the lovely silver birch a Betula Pendula, the beautiful flowering apple tree a Malis Domestica and the stately chestnut tree an Aesculus Hippocastanum. Then they wonder why the ladies don't find them fascinating.

Can you sing "Reproductive conkers cast off by an Aesculus Hippocastanum roasting on an open fire?"

    Philosophilus

I must concede that physicists are not as bad off as botanists. They bandy about terms like bosons, leptons and quarks. Nobody knows what those are, but at least they're pronounceable.

    Philosophilus

Despite their totally unintelligible utterances, doctors, for some reason, are highly sought after by the ladies. But, technically, they are practitioners, not scientists. And, it has been said that money speaks louder than words.

    Philosophilus

With the passage of time, man has progressively lost the ability to create things of enduring value. The wheel, which was created eons before the dawn of history is still very much in vogue. The abacus was used for some four millennia before being outmoded by the calculator. Whale oil lanterns were used for generations before being replaced by gas, which, in turn, was quickly replaced by electricity. The latest tablet computer is obsolete in nanoseconds.

Philosophilus

The world has been going to hell for a very long time. Indeed, the whole earth has been getting progressively warmer for thousands of years. If we were to undo this phenomenon, we'd have to find the means to create a massive wall of ice across a place called Ohio.

The people of Ohio might not like that.

Philosophilus

In ancient times, the intellectual pursuits now known as science and philosophy were considered as a single discipline. Modern man has demoted them into separate unrelated disciplines to the detriment of both.

Philosophilus

Despite man's custom of accepting them as such, scientific observations are not facts. Indeed, every scientific observation, by its very nature, is at least twice removed from being a fact. This is because a scientific observation is nothing more than an interpretation of the phenomena which happened to be detected in an experiment.

First, there is no way to determine if the apparatus used in the experiment detected everything required to understand the phenomena being examined and there is no way to determine the significance of whatever was not detected.

Second, an interpretation is the result of a human decision process. That process is guided by what we know, which is just another word for what we believe. What we believe is a function of previous interpretations of previous experiences. Even those beliefs which reside in generally accepted theory are nothing more than previous interpretations of the phenomena detected in previous experiments. Other beliefs reside both unknown and, therefore, unexamined in our subconscious. But the fact that we are unaware of them does not mean they don't influence our decisions. What it does mean is that we have no way of knowing what the effect of that influence is.

Because they are at least twice removed from fact, scientific observations do not prove anything. What they do is indicate what may be true, given available information and subject to the validity of its interpretation. This is why a true scientist considers everything he knows to be open to question. This limitation results directly from the human condition and will continue for as long as we remain human.

Philosophilus

The hallmarks of a scientist who understands the human condition are humility and an open mind.

Philosophilus

On Cosmology

I understand that the wizards of modern times have concocted a theory that the entire universe and everything in it blew up from nothing. No, I won't repeat that; you'll just have to read it again. As a result of this great explosion, or Big Bang, everything is reported to be racing madly away from everything else. Except, they tell us, where there is something they call a Black Hole.

A Black Hole is created when the enormous mass of an exploding star, whose atoms are all rushing madly away from each other, changes its mind and, instead, collapses everything together. Because its mass is so great, the miniscule point where everything crunches together has an unimaginably strong gravitational field. The gravity is so strong that the Black Hole gobbles up nearby stars and even galaxies, packing them all together. This packs everything

so tightly that, allegedly, it ceases to exist, at least as we are able to comprehend existence.

Many strange things are said to happen in a Black Hole. Even something called a photon, which is said to be a tiny spark of energy called light, is crushed into virtually, if not even absolutely, nothing. Because it has no mass, the photon normally can race off at the speed of light. This is a good thing, since if a photon is light it must be able to keep up with itself.

Some scientists even claim that a photon is a photon only when it is mediating an interaction between particles, whatever that means. When they are packed as tightly as they are in a Black Hole, they can't even wiggle, let alone mediate an interaction. Apparently, they are so annoyed by the circumstances in which they find themselves that they go over to the Dark Side. That's probably why a Black Hole is such a black hole.

The theory of the Big Bang holds that everything now spread out all over the universe once was all crunched together in a really, really tiny point at the center of the granddaddy of all Black Holes. It was packed so tight that even a lot of the things scientists now call particles didn't have room to exist. And, as I've explained, photons didn't have enough wiggle room to mediate an interaction and had gone to the Dark Side, probably in a sulk. No one knows how long it sat there that way, because time, apparently, didn't yet exist. But it must have seemed like a long time since nothing was having any fun.

At any rate, eventually in the passage of non-time, something or someone tweaked a photon and caused it to mediate an interaction. The energy released must have stimulated another photon into action, and so on. With everything packed so tightly in such a small space, you can see how this might cascade into a massive release of energy. That not only might make a big bang but even a Big Bang, making everything race off madly in all directions to create the universe we have all grown to know and love.

I can just imagine the kind of prankster who would do such a thing saying something ironic like "Let there be light!"

Philosophilus

On the Meaning of Life

The beauty of a sunset, the joy of fresh air laden with the scent of growing things and the endless bounty man receives from the wondrous earth of divine creation brings me to the very brink of gratitude for the love and generosity of a benevolent God. However, I also am mindful that when we gain enough wisdom to stop making hilarious blunders in our attempts to deal with the vicissitudes of life, we are brought into demise and a new crop of inexperienced players is brought onstage.

Philosophilus

If you feel you've been enrolled without your knowledge or consent in a mandatory boarding school which has no published curriculum or scheduled lectures and you are being subjected to unannounced exams upon which your very existence may depend, you have my congratulations. You're achieving a higher state of awareness.

        Philosophilus

People often believe that life is capricious. All kinds of things just happen, willy nilly. Actually, life is permeated by subtle linkages that maintain a cosmic balance. For example, as you grow older, your waistline increases but your inseam decreases, thus maintaining a balance in total measurements.

        Philosophilus

The supreme moral value that our conscience attributes to living things is self-evident, but also is challenged by a world in which every living thing can survive only by consuming other living things. Even vegans consume other living things.

This is what we call a conundrum.

        Philosophilus

Surviving by consuming other living things

After extensive cogitation on the nature of being, and copious observations of the nature of nature, I have deduced, induced and adduced that the purpose of life is to persevere.

For life to persevere, the individual beings possessed by and in possession of the spark of life must persevere and procreate.

It is the duty of the plant, the insect, the spider, the bird and whatever it is that's climbing up the tree to persevere and procreate.

Man, being in possession of sentience, has additional duties. The duties of man are to think, to learn, to dream great dreams, to grow intellectually, emotionally and spiritually, to study nature and the universe, to recognize that he is but a part of the grand scheme of life, to have reverence for the creator of life and for his own being, and to treat with respect and kindness every other form of life within the limits of his duty to persevere and procreate.

      Philosophilus

On This and That

If the purveyors of periodical publications were to bill for renewals any earlier than they do, we'd be inundated with panicky pleas for renewal before having submitted our initial subscriptions.

Philosophilus

If you find gum under your seat, leave it alone.

Philosophilus

Considering some of the stuff western man asks the Chinese to manufacture for him, it's no wonder they think that Occidentals have neither taste nor common sense.

Philosophilus

Do not mourn the passing of an era. Remember what a bother and nuisance it was and celebrate the birth of the new one.

Philosophilus

One man's subtle is another man's obtuse.

Philosophilus

As much as we may loathe the experience of change, we can make progress only by changing something.

My condolences.
Philosophilus

Sleeping on a difficult decision does not improve the decision, but it does provide the benefit of delaying the inevitable.
Philosophilus

The problem with undergarments is that it doesn't seem to matter if we iron them or not. It does seem to matter, at least eventually, whether we change them or not.
Philosophilus

The most common argument for steadfastly adhering to a failed procedure is that "We've always done it that way."
Philosophilus

So many have mastered the insight that the perfect should not be the enemy of the good that a great many have progressed to the point where the good is not even the enemy of the mediocre.

Philosophilus

Attempting to teach patience to the young is an exercise in futility. Running on a treadmill to lose weight is exercise in futility.

Philosophilus

The thing men hate the most about having their hair trimmed is not the wasteful use of time, it is the futility of it. No matter how elegantly one's hair is trimmed, in just a few months it's a mess.

Philosophilus

The difference between predator and prey is a matter of mindset. If you find yourself in the presence of a dangerous animal and you are not the predator, I have some bad news for you.

Philosophilus

There are those who say that when faced with a dangerous predator you should calmly stare it down, thereby demonstrating that you are not prey. There are others, perhaps wiser, who say you should never waste valuable time looking a predator in the eye. It should only see your backside receding rapidly into the distance.

Philosophilus

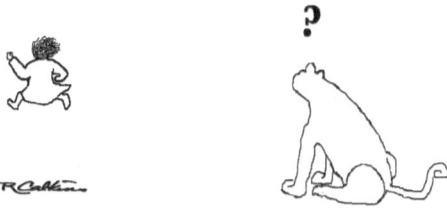

Having ideas so good that they are stolen by others can be a source of pride. It can also be a source of poverty.

Philosophilus

Even in ancient times the breadth of knowledge became so great that we were forced to specialize. For example, a misanthrope is a generalist, whereas a misogynist is a specialist. As a philosopher, of course, I was a generalist.

Philosophilus

An old adage is not necessarily better than a new one. It just got thought of first.

Philosophilus

Philosophers have long pondered why it is that inanimate objects, when dropped, display an uncanny ability to run under furniture.

They also are much puzzled by the fact that the smaller and more important the object, the farther it can run.

Philosophilus

PHILOSOPHILUS' LAW OF REGRESSION

The reason all things eventually go to pot is because there are more ways to screw things up than there are to fix them.

COMING SOON FROM ADP A DIFFERENT PERCEPTION

ONELINERS

In this fun and easy-to-read book, you'll learn how to use the power of the line to identify and empower objects, both animate and inanimate. You'll learn how a single line not only can communicate actions and emotions, but even can tell a story. You'll even learn how the entire universe could be captured on a single, unbroken line. The power of the line is truly immense for those who understand it.

To demonstrate each concept as forcefully as possible, every illustration in the book is drawn with a single, unbroken line. That line never crosses nor even touches itself from beginning to end, hence, the term "oneliners". Everything you see, think and feel about each illustration is caused by the characteristics of that single line. That line is the only thing that's there. The purity of this approach and the challenge of creating every illustration with a single, unbroken line make this book unique. It takes you from simple examples to complete drawings.

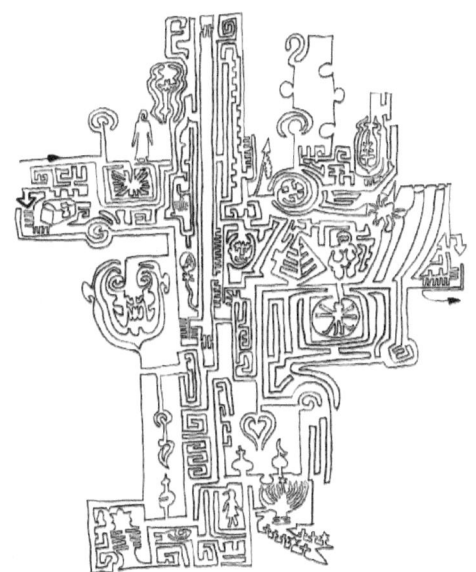

THE CATACOMBS OF SECRETS AND SYMBOLS

A BEAR IN YOUR FACE

SAILING ON A WINDY DAY

For more information about ADP A Different Perception go to calkinspublishing.com

www.ingramcontent.com/pod-product-compliance
Lightning Source LLC
Chambersburg PA
CBHW020701300426
44112CB00007B/472